Appetizer/Cocktail Recipes

for sharing

bite your
tongue

Est. 2002

Authentic New Orleans Cuisine

po boys + catering + heat & eat

Contents

APPETIZERS

COCKTAILS

CHARCUTERIE

Appetizers

ap·pe·tiz·er

A noun

A small dish of food or a drink taken
before a meal or the main course of
a meal to stimulate one's appetite.

Notes

Crabmeat Deviled Eggs 4 Servings

Ingredients

6 hard-boiled eggs, yolks smashed in a bowl
4 tablespoons mayonnaise
1 tablespoon of Creole Mustard
¼ cup crabmeat
2 teaspoons chopped green onions
1 teaspoons capers
fresh lemon juice
salt and pepper
paprika

Preparation

Combine the mashed egg yolks with the mayonnaise and Creole mustard. Gently stir in the crabmeat, green onions, capers and lemon juice. Season with salt and pepper. Fill the egg whites evenly with the mixture and garnish with paprika. Serve at room temperature or lightly chilled.

bite your tongue
Authentic New Orleans Cuisine

Notes

Ingredients

5 fresh tomatoes; diced
1 4oz can of green chiles
1 can whole tomatoes with juice
½ cup cilantro leaves
¼ cup chopped onion
1 clove garlic
1 jalapeno
¼ teaspoon cumin
¼ teaspoon salt
¼ teaspoon sugar
½ lime, for juice

Preparation

Combine all the ingredients and gently stir/fold.

bite your
tongue
Est. 2002
Authentic New Orleans Cuisine
po boys + catering + heat & eat

Restaurant Style Salsa 4 Servings

Notes

Marinated Olives with Rosemary, Garlic and Lemon

4 Servings

Ingredients

1 pound of assorted olives
4 teaspoon chopped garlic
4 sprigs fresh rosemary
8 sprigs fresh thyme
2 bay leaves
4 lemon slices
1 teaspoon crushed red pepper flakes
1 cup olive oil

Preparation

Assemble: Layer the olives, garlic, herbs, bay leaf, lemon slices and red pepper flakes in a glass bowl. Pour the olive oil over top, just until the olives are submerged. Then refrigerate.

Serve: 2 hours before serving, remove the olives from the refrigerator to bring them to room temperature. Transfer to your favorite serving bowl. Enjoy them on their own or serve along with crackers, charcuterie or on a holiday cheese board.

bite your tongue
Authentic New Orleans Cuisine

Notes

Ingredients

1-8 inch flour tortilla
1/3 cup shredded Havarti cheese
2 teaspoon chopped; toasted pecans
pear preserves

Preparation

Sprinkle one side of the tortilla with the cheese and nuts. Fold the tortilla. Coat a nonstick skillet with vegetable cooking spray and cook quesadilla over medium-high heat for 2 minutes on each side or until cheese melts. Remove from heat, slice into wedges and serve with pear preserves on the side.

bite your tongue
Est. 2002
Authentic New Orleans Cuisine
po boys + catering + heat & eat

Pecan Havarti Quesadilla with Pear Preserves

1 Serving

Notes

_____

_____

_____

_____

_____

_____

_____

_____

_____

_____

Ingredients

Blue Cheese Dip:

1 ½ cups mayonnaise
½ cup packed blue cheese crumbles
½ teaspoon hot sauce
2 teaspoons of Worcestershire sauce
1 teaspoon salt
½ lemon juice
1 teaspoon chopped garlic

Preparation

To make the sauce, combine all ingredients in a large bowl and adjust the seasoning if necessary. Serve the chicken alongside the dipping sauce. (See next page for sauce recipe)

Buffalo Chicken Cheese Balls 15-20 Servings

Ingredients

Chicken Balls:

1 store-bought rotisserie chicken
¼ cup hot sauce – recommended: Frank's Red Hot
1 teaspoon ground black pepper
1 ¾ cups sharp cheddar
¼ cup sliced green onions
1 cup all purpose flour
3 eggs, lightly beaten
2 cups panko bread crumbs
vegetable oil, for frying

Preparation

Heat the deep fryer to 350 degrees F.

Pick the meat from the chicken and discard the skin. Place the chicken in a large bowl and add the hot sauce, pepper cheese and green onions and toss to combine. Roll the chicken into 2-ounce balls, about the size of a golf ball.

Place the flour, eggs and bread crumbs in 3 separate bowls. Roll each ball in the flour, then the egg and then the bread crumbles. Set aside.

When the oil is hot, fry the chicken balls in batches. Cook for about 2 minutes per batch. Remove the chicken to paper towel lined plate to drain the excess oil.

Notes

Ingredients

vegetable oil, for frying
2 cup all-purpose flour
¼ cup cornstarch
2 teaspoons kosher salt
1 teaspoon creole seasoning
½ teaspoon paprika
½ teaspoon garlic powder
1 cup buttermilk
1 egg
1 (16 oz) jar dill pickle chips, drained and patted dry
Ranch Dressing

bite your tongue
Est. 2002
Authentic New Orleans Cuisine
po boys + catering + heat & eat

Preparation

Heat ¾ inch of vegetable oil in a large cast iron skillet until a deep fry thermometer reaches 375 degrees.
In a wide, shallow bowl, mix together the flour, cornstarch, salt, creole seasoning, paprika and garlic powder. In a separate wide, shallow bowl, whisk the buttermilk and egg to combine. Place ¼ of the pickle slices in the buttermilk mixture and gently stir with a fork to coat. Using a slotted spoon, drain the pickles well, place them in the flour mixture and toss to combine. Add pickles to the skillet and fry until golden brown and crispy, about 2 minutes. Using a clean slotted spoon, transfer the pickles to a paper towel-lined plate. Repeat with the remaining 3 batches of pickles. Serve immediately with ranch dressing for dipping.

New Orleans Fried Pickles

1 Serving

Notes

Alix's Queso with Chorizo 6-8 Servings

Ingredients

1 pound chorizo. Beef or pork
1 diced onion finely chopped & sautéed
½ pound Velveeta cheese block
1 can diced tomatoes and green chiles
2 cans chopped green chiles
1 jalapeno, diced
½ bunch cilantro, garnish
tortilla chips

Preparation

Sautee the onion and sausage in a large nonstick skillet, breaking the sausage up as you go. Once cooked, drain off the fat. Chop the cheese block into cubes and add along with the diced tomatoes and green chiles and chopped green chiles, juice and all. Cook over a low heat until it all starts coming together. Then stir in the diced jalapenos. Serve with chips.

Authentic New Orleans Cuisine | 15

Notes

Ingredients

1-12oz Zatarain's Dirty Rice Mix
1 pound ground spicy pork sausage
6 eggs; scrambled
1 tablespoon Zatarain's Creole Seasoning
10 flour tortillas
sour cream
salsa
shredded monterey jack cheese
fresh cilantro, chopped
1 onion, finely diced and sauteed

Preparation

Sautee the onion in tablespoons of butter; set aside. Prepare Zatarain's dirty rice mix according to package and instructions substituting ground sausage for ground beef. Fold the scrambled eggs, onion and creole seasoning into the dirty rice mix. Fill tortillas with rice mixture and cheese. Garnish with sour cream, salsa and cilantro.

bite your tongue
Est. 2002
Authentic New Orleans Cuisine
po boys + catering + heat & eat

Authentic New Orleans Style Wraps 10 Servings

Cocktails

A cocktail is an alcoholic mixed drink. Most commonly, cocktails are either a combination of spirits, or one or more spirits mixed with other ingredients such as tonic water, fruit juice, flavored syrup, or cream.

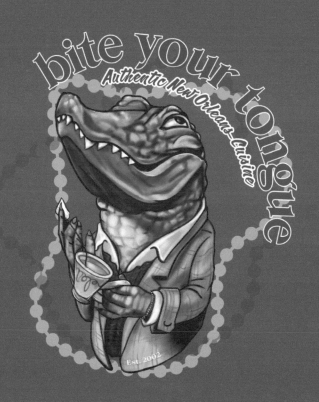

Notes

Strawberry Hennessy Margaritas 2 Servings

Ingredients

1 pint fresh strawberries
¼ cup water
¼ cup granulated sugar
2 cups ice
½ lime juiced
2 tablespoons Hennessy Cognac
2 tablespoons Grand Marnier

Preparation

Place strawberries, water, and sugar into a blender. Blend until smooth. Strain into a measuring cup to remove the seeds. Add ice, strained strawberry puree, lime juice, Hennessy, and Grand Marnier to blender. Blend until smooth. Pour into glasses. Garnish with strawberry and lime. Serve immediately.

Notes

Ingredients

¾ cup spiced rum
½ cup orange juice
¼ cup banana liqueur
3 cups frozen pineapple orange slices

Preparation

Combine the rum, orange juice, banana liqueur and frozen pineapple in a blender and process until a smoothie consistency. Add more frozen pineapple if too thin and add more orange juice if too thick. Garnish with orange slices

bite your
tongue
Est. 2002
Authentic New Orleans Cuisine
po boys + catering + heat & eat

Everybody Loves The Sunshine 4 Servings

Notes

_____

_____

_____

_____

_____

_____

_____

_____

_____

_____

_____

_____

Preparation

Place first 6 ingredients in large pot.
Add enough water just to cover (about
6 cups). Bring to boil; reduce heat to medium and simmer uncovered until vegetables are very soft, about 50 minutes.
Discard bay leaf. Add 1 tablespoon coarse salt and lemon juice; cool slightly. Working in batches, puree vegetable mixture in blender until smooth. Add enough water, if needed, to measure 8 cups. Cover and chill.

Grind celery seeds with remaining 1 ½ teaspoons coarse salt in mortar with pestle or in spice grinder. Add celery seed salt, Worcestershire sauce, hot sauce, horseradish, black pepper, Tabasco and Guinness, if desired, to vegetable puree. Cover and chill Bloody Mary mix overnight.

Stir Bloody Mary mix and vodka or gin in large pitcher. Fill tall glasses with ice. Divide Bloody Mary among glasses. Garnish with lime wedges

The Best Bloody Mary 8 Servings

Ingredients

1 ½ pounds plum tomatoes, coarsely chopped
1 large carrot, peeled, coarsely chopped
1 large golden beet, peeled, coarsely chopped
1 small fennel bulb, trimmed, coarsely chopped
1 large garlic clove, chopped
1 bay leaf
1 tablespoon plus 1 1/2 teaspoons coarse kosher salt
3 tablespoons fresh lemon juice
½ teaspoon celery seeds
6 tablespoons Worcestershire sauce
1 tablespoon Crystal hot sauce
1 tablespoon prepared horseradish
2 teaspoons coarsely ground whole black peppercorns
1 teaspoon of Tabasco
¼ cup of Guinness beer (optional)
3 cups of vodka or gin
ice cubes
lime wedges

Notes

Ingredients

1 small scoop of ice
1 oz blackberry brandy
2 oz Rose's lime juice
1 oz light rum
1 oz crème de noyaux
3 ½ oz orange juice
1 oz dark rum
1 oz triple sec
3 ½ oz pineapple juice
1 oz Southern Comfort peach liqueur
1 oz grenadine syrup
1 oz banana liqueur
2 oz pina colada mix

Preparation

Shake and pour into a large glass. Garnish with lime slices, orange slices and cherries.

bite your tongue
Est. 2002
Authentic New Orleans Cuisine
po boys + catering + heat & eat

Mardi Gras Mambo 3 Servings

Notes

Strawberry & Lime Moscato Punch 8 Servings

Ingredients

8 cups of Moscato wine
1 can frozen limeade concentrate, defrosted
1 c. strawberries, diced plus 1 c. strawberries, sliced
1 lime, sliced
2 liter 7 up

Preparation

Place 1 cup of diced strawberries and ¼ cup of limeade in a blender and puree. Run through a strainer to remove most of the seeds. Pour into a pitcher, add remaining limeade and Moscato into pitcher, garnish with strawberry and lime slices. Chill in fridge, when ready to serve, top each glass with 7 up.

Notes

Ingredients

2 cups frozen peaches
2 cups lemon-flavored rum – recommended: Bacardi Limon
3 cups peach nectar – recommended: Kerns
1 cup pineapple juice
1 cup ginger ale
2 oz grenadine
1 cup Cran-Pineapple juice

Preparation

Chill all ingredients. Combine all ingredients in a punch bowl, adding ginger ale last. Serve cold.

bite your tongue
Est. 2002
Authentic New Orleans Cuisine
po boys + catering + heat & eat

NOLA Peach Rum Punch 14 Servings

Notes

Adult "Capri Sun" 4-6 Servings

Ingredients

1 can of frozen lemonade
2 oz of cranberry juice
12 oz Hawaiian Punch
¼ liter ginger ale
12 oz pineapple juice
2 lemons
¼ cup citron vodka
¼ cup vodka
4 oz Triple Sec
4 oz grenadine
4 by 6 zipper bags

Preparation

Slice both lemons for garnish. Mix all ingredients. Pour portions into zipper bags. Punch a hole/insert straw

Notes

Ingredients

4 oz New Orleans Strango
2 oz Tito's vodka
1 Strawberry

Preparation

Mix Strango and Tito's vodka in a shaker. Add a few cubes of ice and shake well. Pour into a Martini glass and garnish with a sliced strawberry.

Note: Strango is a blend of strawberry, lemonade and mango tea. Pairs well with your favorite spirit!

bite your
tongue
Est. 2002
Authentic New Orleans Cuisine
po boys + catering + heat & eat

Stradka (Strango + Vodka) 1 Serving

Notes

Hennessy Margarita _{1 Serving}

Ingredients

2 cups ice
2 oz Hennessy Cognac
1.5 oz Tequila
1.5 oz Triple Sec
3 oz Sweet & Sour Mix
Tajin
¼ Lime

Preparation

Take a lime and cut it into fourths. Take one wedge and rub the rim of your glass with the juice of your lime. Place the top of your glass in tajin, or salt to rim and garnish your glass. Set aside. Take a cocktail shaker and fill it with ice. Add Hennessy, tequila, triple sec, and sweet and sour mix to your cocktail shaker. Shake vigorously. Pour into a cocktail glass, garnish with a lime wedge.

Notes

Ingredients

¼ cup vanilla extract
¼ cup sugar
¼ cup water
2 inch piece of ginger (peeled and chopped)
½ vanilla bean (split and seeds scraped)
2 cups fresh pineapple juice
3 cups fresh pineapple juice (poured into ice cubes trays and frozen)
¼ cup vanilla vodka
mint sprigs
pineapple slices

bite your tongue
Est. 2002
Authentic New Orleans Cuisine
po boys • catering • heat & eat

Preparation

Combine the sugar, water, ginger and vanilla bean and seeds in a small saucepan over medium heat and bring to a boil. Cook the mixture until the sugar is completely dissolved, about 1 minute. Cool at room temperature and strain.

Combine the pineapple juice, 1 cup of pineapple cubes, the simple syrup and vodka in a blender and blend until smooth. Pour into glasses filled with pineapple cubes, if desired, and garnish with mint and pineapple slices.

Pineapple Ginger Vanilla Vodka 4-6 Servings

Notes

Golden Pecan Martini 1 Serving

Ingredients

1 ½ oz pecan liqueur
2 teaspoons Louisiana pecan meal (finely ground pecans)
2 oz vodka, chilled
Pecans

Preparation

Put ½ oz of the pecan liqueur into a small dish. Add the pecan meal to another small dish. Dip the rim of a chilled martini glass first in the pecan liqueur, then in the pecan meal. Add the remaining pecan liqueur and the vodka to the glass and drop in the pecan half. Serve immediately.

Authentic New Orleans Cuisine | 41

Notes

Ingredients

1 cup fresh lime juice
2 cups grenadine syrup
2 cups Jamaican white rum
1 cup light rum
2 cups fresh pineapple juice
2 cups fresh orange juice
orange slices
pineapple slices

Preparation

Mix all ingredients together in a pitcher or punch bowl. Chill in the refrigerator for at least 1 hour before serving. Garnish with orange or pineapple slices.

bite your
tongue

Est. 2002

Authentic New Orleans Cuisine

po boys + catering + heat & eat

New Orleans Rum Punch 8-10 Servings

Notes

Moscow Mule 1 Serving

Ingredients

½ oz lime juice
2 oz vodka
4 oz ginger beer
lime

Preparation

Mix lime juice, vodka, ginger beer. Add ice, stir, and garnish with a fresh lime wedge.

Notes

Ingredients

8 oz pineapple
8 teaspoons honey
chopped mint leaves
2 lemons, juiced
16 oz seltzer
4 oz limoncello

Preparation

Add a piece of pineapple, 2 teaspoons Honey Simple Syrup, and 1 teaspoon chopped mint to each of 4 tall glasses and muddle. Fill half of each glass with ice. In a pitcher, mix together the lemon juice, seltzer and limoncello, if using. Divide the mixture among the glasses and garnish with fresh pineapple and mint sprigs.

Honey Simple Syrup

Ingredients

4 tablespoons water
4 tablespoons honey

Preparation

Heat the water and honey in a small pot over low heat. When the mixture is hot remove it from the heat and let cool.

Pineapple Honey Cordial 4 Servings

Notes

Frozen Tangerine Margaritas 1 Serving

Ingredients

2 oz Tequila
1 oz orange liqueur – recommended: Cointreau
½ oz fresh tangerine juice
½ oz fresh lime juice
salt, optional

Preparation

Combine Tequila, orange liqueur, tangerine liqueur, lime juice, and ice, in a blender and blend until smooth. Line rims of glasses with salt, if desired. Divide margaritas among glasses, and serve. To serve margaritas straight up, combine all ingredients, except salt, in a shaker. Strain into glasses and serve.

Notes

Ingredients

7 cups strawberries, hulled
1 ¼ cups chopped fresh mint leaves
5 tablespoons agave nectar
1 cup fresh lime juice
¼ cup rum, optional
2 cups seltzer water
special equipment: ice pop molds

Preparation

Cut 6 cups strawberries in half, then slice the remaining 1 cup strawberries. Divide the sliced strawberries among 18 (3-ounce) pop molds. Set the Halved strawberries aside.

In a blender, combine the remaining strawberries and mint leaves, agave, lime juice and rum, if using. With the motor running, gradually add the seltzer water and blend until the mixture becomes smooth enough to pour.

Divide the mixture among the prepared molds and top with the remaining ¼ cup mint. Add the ice pop sticks to the molds. Freeze 4 to 6 hours or until solid.

Strawberry Mojito Ice Pops

18 Servings

Charcuterie

Charcuterie is a French term for a branch of cooking devoted to prepared meat products, such as bacon, ham, sausage, terrines, galantines, ballotines, pâtés, and confit, primarily from pork. Charcuterie is part of the garde manger chef's repertoire.

Notes

Martine's Charcuterie Board

4-6 Servings

Ingredients

Cheeses: (choose 3,5,7 (depending on party size) hard cheeses and soft cheeses

Meats: Cured meats like prosciutto, salami, ham, chorizo, capricola or soppressata
Savory Accompaniments: Nuts, olives, savory dips and spreads, cold cut veggies

Sweet Accompaniments: Fresh fruit and berries, dried fruit, sweet spreads, chocolate

Crackers: Pita, whole grain, toasted baguettes or mini toasts crackers

Preparation

1. Choose your board depending on party size
2. Start with the cheese
3. Fold and add meats
4. Add savory and sweet accompaniments

Enjoy!

I love entertaining at home and these recipes have been prepared over the years for my family and friends. These are the most popular ones in my repertoire.

Growing up in New Orleans, food is always at the center of any celebration. Appetizers and Cocktails will always lead the way and be the opening act of the occasion.

~

Chef Martine

Martine Courtney Clark

Chef Martine is from New Orleans, LA. She and her family evacuated to Charlotte a day before hurricane Katrina in 2005. Following the breach in the levees, she decided to make Charlotte her home. In New Orleans, she opened Bite Your Tongue Take Out and Catering in 2002. She began offering Charlotte a taste of N'awlins cuisine in June of 2007. She has had much success in the restaurant and catering business in the Queen City. The white chocolate bread pudding, seafood gumbo "Lulu" and her signature drink "Strango," are her most popular food items. In 2017, she started at 73 & Main & her love for cooking continued. On Nov 9th, 2021, she ventured out again with the "New" Bite Your Tongue take out, delivery and catering. During the Mardi Gras season she prepares gumbo, jambalaya and red beans & rice. It has been her pleasure bringing a taste of NOLA to the Queen City! She is the proud mother of two: Lucius Jr., and Alix. She also has two grand kids: Lucius III and Luna.

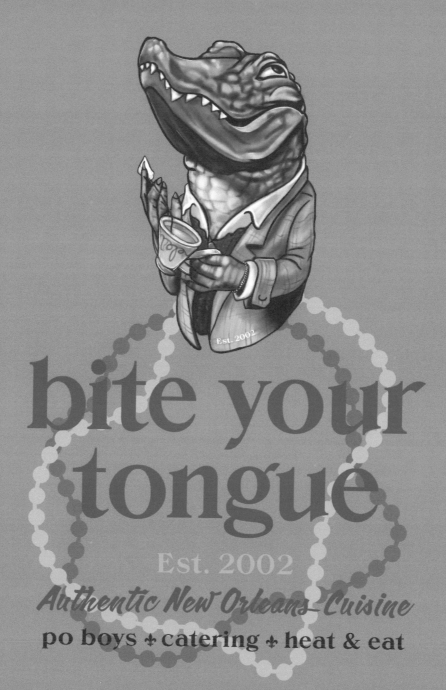

bite your
tongue

Est. 2002

Authentic New Orleans Cuisine

po boys ⚜ catering ⚜ heat & eat

http://www.NewBiteYourTongue.com

Printed in the USA
CPSIA information can be obtained
at www.ICGtesting.com
LVHW061801021023
759809LV00018B/128